W9-CRK-470

IKIGAI

生き甲斐

To my dear husband,
Our life together is my ikigai and will
always be an adventure.

Calligraphy by
RIE TAKEDA

YUKARI
MITSUHASHI

IKIGAI

giving every day
meaning and joy

KYLE BOOKS

An Hachette UK Company
www.hachette.co.uk

First published in Great Britain in 2018 by

Kyle Books, an imprint of Kyle Cathie Ltd
Carmelite House
50 Victoria Embankment
London EC4Y 0DZ

www.kylebooks.co.uk
ISBN 978 0 85783 491 1

Text copyright 2018 © Yukari Mitsuhashi
Design and layout copyright 2018 © Kyle Cathie Ltd

Distributed in the US by Hachette Book Group, 1290 Avenue of
the Americas, 4th and 5th Floors, New York, NY 10104

Distributed in Canada by Canadian Manda Group, 664 Annette St.,
Toronto, Ontario, Canada M6S 2C8

Yukari Mitsuhashi is hereby identified as the author of this work in accordance
with Section 77 of the Copyright, Designs and Patents Act 1988.

All rights reserved. No part of this work may be reproduced or utilised
in any form or by any means, electronic or mechanical, including
photocopying, recording or by any information storage and retrieval
system, without the prior written permission of the publisher.

Editor: Tara O'Sullivan
Designer: Nicky Barneby
Calligraphy and cover illustration: Rie Takeda
Production: Lisa Pinnell

A Cataloguing in Publication record for this title is
available from the British Library.

Printed in China

10 9 8 7 6 5 4 3

Contents

INTRODUCTION

IKIGAI

はじめに

Introduction: *Ikigai*

What is *ikigai*? In more than seven years working as a freelance journalist, this has been the most complex subject I have had to explore to date. Until I was commissioned to write an article on *ikigai* for the BBC[1], I took the concept for granted. It is such a common notion — and so deeply engraved in the Japanese psyche — that I never really stopped and thought about what it means.

The Japanese word *ikigai* is formed of two Japanese characters, or *kanji*: 'iki' [生き], meaning life, and 'gai' [甲斐], meaning value or worth. *Ikigai*, then, is the value of life, or happiness in life. Put simply, it's the reason you get up in the morning.

Some recent Western interpretations of *ikigai* may seem to explore the idea of finding a meaning to your life as a whole, but that is not quite what the word means. The English word 'life' carries the sense of both lifetime and daily life, but in Japanese, we have a separate word for each: the former is expressed by '*jinsei*' [人生], while '*seikatsu*' [生活] denotes everyday life. When I spoke to Akihiro Hasegawa, a clinical psychologist and associate professor at Toyo Eiwa University who has studied the concept of *ikigai* for years, he made an interesting point. *Ikigai* translated into English as 'life's purpose' sounds quite formidable, but *ikigai* need not be the one overriding purpose of a person's life. In fact, the word 'life' used here aligns more with *seikatsu* — daily life. In other words, *ikigai* can be about the joy a person finds in living day-to-day, without which their life as a whole would not be a happy one.

The reason the topic of *ikigai* is a difficult one to tackle — even for someone who is Japanese — is because, although it is a common concept in Japan, it is not something you learn from a textbook. Growing up and living in Japan for most of my life, I don't recall ever being taught about *ikigai* in a classroom. Japanese children learn more than 1,000 *kanji* in elementary (primary) school alone, but *ikigai* is not one of them. *Ikigai* is a multifaceted concept that we come to understand as we live life and grow older. 'What is your *ikigai*?' is not a straightforward question with one right answer but an abstract one, to which an infinite number of responses are possible. Whatever gets you up in the morning is your *ikigai* — and no one can tell you otherwise.

Since there are no *ikigai* teachers, I undertook my own exploration on the concept, which I share with you in this book. In the coming chapters, we will explore what *ikigai* means, how to discover your own *ikigai*, and how doing so can help to bring focus and joy to your life. I am grateful to the experts in different fields who have provided me with their insights, as well as to the people who have shared their *ikigai* with me (see chapter five for some inspiring stories). Everyone's *ikigai* is different, but my hope is that reading about other people's stories will help you to discover your own.

Life will always come at you with its own set of difficulties and *ikigai* is by no means a magic formula that makes things perfect. But by having *ikigai* at each stage in our lives, hopefully we can look back at our life as a whole and feel content. I hope that my search to better grasp the Japanese notion of *ikigai* will

生き甲斐

help you not only to understand it, too, but also — and more importantly — will inspire you to think about your own *ikigai*. Thank you for joining me on this journey. Whatever *ikigai* you may find at the end of this book, I say '*kanpai*' (cheers) to that!

CHAPTER 1

WHAT IS IKIGAI!?

生き甲斐とは

What is *ikigai*?

It might be the sound of our alarm clock
that forces us awake in the morning, but it's
the joy we anticipate in the day ahead that
gets us up and going. As I explained in the
introduction, the word *ikigai* comes from *iki*,
meaning life, and *gai*, meaning value. So it can
be interpreted as the values in your life that
make it worth living.

According to Professor Hasegawa, the word
ikigai can be traced back to the Heian period
(794–1185 CE). *Gai* comes from the word
kai, which means 'shell', as shells were once
regarded as highly valuable. From there, *ikigai*
is derived as a word that means 'value in living'
or 'values in life'. There are other Japanese
concepts that represent different values,
all ending with *gai*. For example, *hatarakigai*
refers to value in work (*hataraki* or *hataraku*
means 'work' or 'to work'), while *yarigai* refers
to value in what you are doing (*yari* or *yaru*

means 'to do'). *Ikigai*, however, is more of a comprehensive concept.

Because it is related to everyday life, as I explained in the introduction, *ikigai* tends to be pragmatic rather than simply idealistic. A person's *ikigai* might be their family, work or hobby, a photography trip they have planned for the weekend, or even something as simple as a cup of morning coffee enjoyed with their spouse, or taking their dog out for a walk.

The Japanese proverb *jūnin toiro* literally means 'ten people, ten colours': as people are different in their characters, preferences and the way they think, it is only to be expected that ten different people would choose ten different colours when asked which is their favourite. The same is true of *ikigai* as well. Each person's *ikigai* is unique because we all find joy in different aspects of life. There is no right or wrong answer.

Work or pleasure?

A common Western misconception of *ikigai* is that it must be related to your career. Those of you familiar with the concept may have seen explanations of *ikigai* that make use of a

Venn diagram consisting of four overlapping circles — what you love, what you are good at, what the world needs and what you can be paid for — with *ikigai* at the intersection of all four. I first discovered this definition when I was researching *ikigai* for my article for the BBC — and it took me by surprise.

Why? Because it limits the concept of *ikigai* to things related to work: in this narrow definition, your *ikigai* needs to be something you can be paid for. But for Japanese people, *ikigai* is a much broader concept, and one that is rooted in our everyday lives. *Ikigai* might be our work, yes, but it can also be a hobby, our loved ones, or something as simple as enjoying the company of friends. In a survey of 2,000 Japanese men and women conducted by Central Research Services in 2010, just 31 per cent considered work as their *ikigai*[2]. In fact, *ikigai* was most commonly related to a hobby or leisure interest, followed by family and pets or time spent with them. I will explore the idea of *ikigai* at work further in chapter four.

A type of happiness?

When you consider the idea of such *ikigai* as time spent with family or enjoying hobbies, you might think that *ikigai* is just another word for happiness. In Japanese, the word for happiness is *shiawase* or *kōfuku*. So how are *shiawase* and *ikigai* different?

In her definitive book on the concept of *ikigai*, Japanese author and psychiatrist Mieko Kamiya defines *ikigai* as a *type* of happiness[3]. But, according to Kamiya, perhaps the main difference between *shiawase* and *ikigai* is that *ikigai* carries with it the idea of moving towards the future. If you have a goal or something to look forward to, then — even if you feel that you're not in a good place right now — you are more likely to be able to see your current situation or circumstances as a pathway towards that future and to find value in the present moment.

Japanese culture and *ikigai*

Although the concept of *ikigai* might be so familiar to Japanese people as to be something we rarely actually discuss, we are reminded,

生き甲斐とは

through our language and our culture, of the importance of the joy that is found in everyday life and that we believe will result in a fulfilling life as a whole. There is a strong focus in Japanese culture on paying attention to the present moment. By exploring some examples of this tendency, hopefully you can understand more clearly why the word *ikigai* exists in Japanese culture and not in others.

Attention to the present moment

In the last few years, there has been an increasing focus globally on mindfulness or 'living in the moment'. Popular blogs, bestselling books and wellness experts all emphasize its advantages. For many of us, especially when we're young, life seems to offer so much to explore that it can be hard to sit still. We live like tuna fish — as though we would die if we were to stop moving! While the Japanese are no exception to this habit — many love to keep busy and are always looking for the next thing — we are known for our attention to detail, which I believe allows us to enjoy each moment by being more aware of our surroundings. And *ikigai* is about focussing on individual moments, not just on

生き甲斐

the big journey of life. This attention to and appreciation of the present moment can be found in Japanese culture in many forms.

Take, for example, how the Japanese language addresses time. When speaking about days in the future in English, we use the word 'tomorrow', or talk about 'the day after tomorrow' or 'two days from now', but Japanese has specific words for each day: *ashita* (tomorrow), *asatte* (the day after tomorrow) and *shiasatte* (two days from now). The beginning of the month is *gessho*, the middle of the month is *chūjyun* and the end of the month is *getsumatsu*. With specific words to reference different times, each time is given its own significance.

Haiku

Haiku poems, very short Japanese poems that consist of 17 syllables, are another example of Japanese attention to detail and the joy that is sought in nature. One of the most well-known haiku poets from the Edo period (1603–1868), Matsuo Bashō, wrote this in 1689:

Shizukesa ya
Iwa ni shimiiru
Semi no koe.

It can be roughly translated as:

Deep silence
penetrating the rock
a cicada's voice.

Many haiku poems shed light on the sounds
made by insects, which give each season its
unique character, and many use *kigo*, which
are words specific to different seasons. We are
all given 365 days a year, but a day in April is
surely different to one in December. Japanese
people consider sounds of insects, such as
crickets chirping in the autumn, as part of
nature, as something there to be enjoyed.
Such sounds can easily be dismissed or can go
unnoticed if you are not present. Haiku poems
illustrate not a special incident or scene but
focus on a moment in everyday life and, like
the Japanese language, remind people of the
preciousness of the present moment.

Transience

Another Japanese word that illustrates the
emphasis that Japanese culture puts on the
moments of daily life is *hakanasa*, which can
be translated as frail, transient, momentary

or short-lived. When something is *hakanai* (a verb form), it is considered beautiful because it can be enjoyed only for a short period of time. A symbol of *hakanasa* is cherry blossom in the springtime. *Hanami* is the word used for the traditional Japanese custom of gathering under the blossom-covered trees to eat, drink and enjoy the breathtaking sight. *Hanami* season is no doubt the most joyful time of the year in Japan, when, wherever you go, you will encounter groups of people enjoying what might be gone by the following day.

When you look at such values and cultures in Japan, it gives us an insight into why the word *ikigai* exists in Japanese. In our everyday lives, whether we are immersing ourselves in nature or devouring traditional Japanese food, paying attention to detail grabs our focus onto what is right in front of us instead of wondering about our to-do lists in our head (which we are all guilty of at times). Our nature of paying attention to detail allows us to enjoy individual moments in our lives, permitting us to find joy and *ikigai* in simple, everyday things.

CHAPTER 2

DEFINING IKIGAI

Defining *ikigai*

If there were ten people, there would be ten different *ikigai*. If ten people wrote their own definition of what *ikigai* means, it might result in ten different explanations.

A person may have more than one *ikigai* at any given time and their *ikigai* may change over time. We find different interests every day, and our source of joy changes accordingly. When I asked a friend of mine, Akiko, about her *ikigai*, she told me that it changed after the birth of her daughter. Up until that point, she explained, her life was a self-oriented one where she prioritized the things that gave her pleasure. However, with a daughter to care for and provide for, she now puts her daughter's needs and desires before her desires, and doing so has given her a new sense of *ikigai*. Remember this when you are exploring your *ikigai* — it is something that will grow and change with you.

生き甲斐

Furthermore, not everyone knows what their *ikigai* is. If you're reading this book, perhaps you're interested in discovering yours. Ultimately, knowing your *ikigai* is about knowing yourself, which takes time and effort. It's worth investing this time and effort, though, because once you understand your *ikigai* you can find ways to pursue it, and you may find that many seemingly unrelated areas of your life end up contributing to it in one way or another. In this chapter, I'll give you some guidelines to consider that may help you to better understand what might make something your *ikigai*.

Common elements of ikigai

After asking many people about their *ikigai*, I began to notice common elements in them. To explain these commonalities, I've used a format of A > B: in other words, whatever a person's *ikigai*, it has a tendency to be more A than B. This list should help you when you are trying to identify your own *ikigai*.

Everyday life > Lifetime

Although it's possible for your *ikigai* to be your one great purpose in life — something that allows you to look forward to the future — remember that we live our lives moment by moment. Even if we are tempted to focus on the events that seem most significant in our lives overall, each major event wouldn't happen without the smaller moments leading up to it. Remembering this can help you to see each moment as significant and valuable. As the saying goes, 'life is what happens when you're busy making other plans'. While it can be good to have a bigger purpose in life — whether personal or work-related — finding attainable *ikigai* in your daily life is important to get you going.

External world > Internal world

Would it be possible to feel alive if no one reacted to what you said or did? Probably not. Being fully alive involves interacting with other people. *Ikigai* is not just something you find within yourself, but is often something that connects you to the outside world. For example, people enjoy hobbies, such as photography or baking, not only for their own sakes but also because they are able to share their experience or what they are good at with others. Work, hobbies and volunteering are all ways in which we connect to the outside world.

Giving > Receiving

One of the most rewarding ways to connect to the outside world — and one that makes us feel profoundly alive — is when we contribute to the lives of others. Giving brings us a sense of fulfillment. For his book *The Blue Zones: Lessons on Living Longer from the People Who've Lived the Longest*, Dan Buettner interviewed centenarians living on the southern Japanese island of Okinawa and noted that *ikigai*, as well as a healthy diet and lifestyle, was a contributing factor to their longevity[4]. When their age is celebrated, older people feel responsible to pass on their wisdom and contribute to the prosperity of younger generations, which gives them a purpose in life in service to their communities. Some people find *ikigai* in the act of volunteering, which is about giving without asking for anything in return (see page 42).

生き甲斐の定義

Fluid > Fixed

People often feel *ikigai* towards something that they can see change and progress in. Parents are fascinated by seeing their children learn new things and grow up day by day; a working person feels alive and motivated in progressing at their job; a retired person might find gardening enjoyable because they see flowers and plants grow and change over time. The change need not be a dramatic one, but we all have an underlying desire to seek and witness progression in our lives. In what areas of your life do you see or seek changes?

Emotional > Logical

An essential element of *ikigai* is that it is based on emotions rather than logic. *Ikigai* is something you feel with your heart rather than something you think with your head. Logic would dictate that having more money would make you happier because it would increase your options in life, and yet a person might have all the money in the world and still feel empty inside. As a freelance journalist, I have the privilege of meeting inspiring people, such as tech entrepreneurs. When I do, I feel so thrilled and excited that I cannot wait to share the story with my audience. It is these emotions that are at the basis of my *ikigai*, not shoulds and shouldn'ts of logical thinking. Your emotions do not lie, and it helps to be true to them when you are searching for your *ikigai*. What arouses a feeling of joy in the depths of your heart is likely to be your *ikigai*.

Specific > Abstract

In order to feel alive and fulfilled, we need reactions and responses from the outside world. You are likely to experience the difference you're making when you are involved with those closest to home. It is great to have a desire to solve world hunger – the world surely needs a solution to that problem – but what about the people in your own neighbourhood who are struggling to survive? Although a grand mission is admirable and, with perseverance, might be achievable, starting small and seeing the impact you're making will enable you to find meaning in what you do and give you a stronger sense of purpose. So you might feel a desire to solve world hunger, but you could help in a more specific way by volunteering at a local food bank. This gives you something tangible to focus on.

Active > Passive

No matter how simple, *ikigai* is almost always accompanied by action. (After all, *ikigai* is what gets you up in the morning.) One of my greatest pleasures since childhood has been reading mystery novels. When I read books by my favourite authors, such as Keigo Higashino or Hideo Yokoyama, I am immersed in their world and cannot help but turn the pages. Reading might not seem the most active hobby, but even here, action is involved: I am seeking out a book I want to read and then finishing it. Without action, there would be no *ikigai*. Ask yourself, what are you actively pursuing (even though no one is asking you to)? Looking back over your life, are there things you have continued to do without conscious effort?

生き甲斐の定義

Memories and dreams

Professor Hasegawa also suggests that
memories and future image (both for yourself
or for loved ones) can serve as one's *ikigai*.
Imagining your future self or picturing
your children grown up can give you hope
and a sense of *ikigai* in the current moment.
He told me: 'Interactions with others or
memorable objects can stimulate the feeling
of *ikigai*. Memories of a lost family member,
or especially for older people, of events or
responsibilities they had when they were
younger can help them feel *ikigai*'.

What *ikigai* brings to your life

You might wonder what difference it makes to have an *ikigai* in your life. As I said at the beginning of this chapter, *ikigai* is about knowing yourself and what you want out of life. You can live happily making decisions based on your feelings or instincts moment by moment. But we all know that time flies by, and in order to make the best of the limited time we are given, having a direction in our life can certainly help us to live a more fulfilling life as a whole.

What *ikigai* brings to you would depend on what your *ikigai* is, but for many, knowing your *ikigai* will allow you to:

- feel happy and content
- find a stable state of mind
- have better control over your day-to-day life
- grow and progress
- find a sense of purpose
- feel more driven and motivated
- become more proactive
- find vitality to live and move forward

All of these things come as a result of knowing what you want and value in life.

But above all, by being aware of what you truly enjoy and are passionate about, *ikigai* brings you focus and direction, and serves as an anchor in your life. With *ikigai* in mind, you will not have to think twice about what matters to you, and hence you will know what to prioritize. We are bombarded with endless decisions to be made day after day, but knowing your *ikigai* will eliminate your insecurities about your decisions and allow you to make better ones. You will find that simple decisions, like how you spend your time, will automatically be made for you when you know your *ikigai*. This aspect of *ikigai* is further demonstrated in chapter five.

生き甲斐の定義

CHAPTER 3

INTERESTS AND *IKIGAI*

興味関心と生き甲斐

Interests and *ikigai*

Curiosity

One common trait I've noticed in Japanese people is that we are very curious! If you visit Tokyo, you will discover signs of Japanese people's curiosity scattered throughout the city. Shoppers queuing outside the doors of newly opened shops or restaurants, and lots of new products on offer at the many 24/7 convenience stores to meet their appetite for new products. For an island that would fit inside the state of California, Japan has very diverse micro-cultures. It is not just Tokyo or Kyoto that have interesting cultures — all 47 prefectures come with their own set of local cultures, whether in food or art.

It can also be said that because Japan is an island, its people have often looked outside of themselves to seek new and interesting ideas. As Pearl S Buck, an American writer,

生き甲斐

once noted: 'The people of Japan have been searchers and discoverers of the best in every culture. Whatever they have learned they have not used imitatively but creatively, taking what was useful to their way of life, changing and adapting and making anew. Their culture is an admirable blend of the best in other cultures and the indigenous culture of her own people.'[5] Buck's observation, made some 50 years ago, remains true today.

Having a curious approach to life can help you discover your *ikigai*: pursuing your curiosity leads to action, which, as we've seen, is a fundamental aspect of *ikigai*.

興味関心と生き甲斐

Hobbies

Many Japanese people pursue their curiosity in the form of hobbies. When I lived in Tokyo, one hobby of mine was to go exploring a secondhand books market called Jimbocho near Tokyo station. With over 170 bookstores in this area alone, I could spend an entire day immersing myself in aisle after aisle of old books. Many of my Japanese friends have interesting hobbies as well. Some play a form of Japanese chess called *shogi*, wearing traditional clothing, *hakama*; another friend goes out to the suburbs to farm at weekends; another enjoys strolling along the streets of Ginza (a high-end shopping area in Tokyo) with her friends, wearing her favourite kimono.

Food as *ikigai*

When you pay attention to the details in your daily life, no matter how ordinary, anything can turn into a memorable experience. Take eating: for most of us, it is something we do three times a day, 365 days a year. But although food is our fuel, and thus a necessity, it can also bring much joy to our lives.

生き甲斐

Japanese people take eating very seriously. There is even a book called *Oishii! Can be Ikigai* (*Delicious! can be ikigai*) written by a 92-year-old celebrity chef, explaining that good food can bring true joy. In his book *Bending Adversity: Japan and the Art of Survival*[6], David Pilling writes 'Slowly I discovered that almost everything the Japanese prepared, however unfamiliar, was fresh and delicious — better, in fact, than any food I had tasted before'. The never-ending curiosity of the Japanese people and the attention they pay to everyday things have made the act of eating an enjoyable experience for them — and their cuisine famous worldwide.

興味関心と生き甲斐

Sharing your *ikigai*

Although hobbies may, at first glance, seem like something you do for your own enjoyment, the truth is they create a way for you to connect, share and contribute to the outside world. Whether you bake, sew, paint or teach, sharing your *ikigai* helps you to connect with others and feel fulfilled.

One of my all-time favourite TV programmes is *The Great British Bake Off*. Unlike some made-in-Hollywood food shows that have clearly been scripted, *GBBO* puts a spotlight on ordinary people who love baking and excel at it. When they bake, they must think of those for whom they're baking and the smile that will appear on their faces as they bite into the food.

Ikigai at every age

Japan is well-known for the longer life expectancy of its inhabitants. My husband, Nick, is American, but after living in Japan for more than three years he noticed that older people there are very active. When you visit traditional Japanese gardens or go hiking, you are likely to encounter older people, either in groups or pairs, walking around, and often taking photos. They often have serious equipment too, making them harder to miss. In a survey of 1,000 Japanese men and women aged 50–79, roughly 60 per cent cited a hobby as their *ikigai*[7]. Specific hobbies they wanted to pursue included things like travelling across Japan by train or learning to dance flamenco.

For them, their hobbies are not just a tool to keep themselves active but a way to share their joy with their loved ones and friends. Whatever your age, finding *ikigai* in the form of hobbies or other activities will get you going and keep you active.

Volunteering as *ikigai*

I've previously mentioned that people may see their *ikigai* as being family, pets, their work or a hobby. But there are other things that it can be too. Professor Hasegawa suggests potential *ikigai* including roles (or responsibility), health, education, experiences, events and memory.

For example, giving up time and energy to volunteer on projects serving the community can also serve as *ikigai*. Kaya Doi, the author and illustrator of the adorable children's book *Chirri & Chirra* (available in English), has devoted her free time to eliminating cruelty to animals for the past ten years. She did this by starting a free paper filled with illustrations to raise awareness and reach more people. She told me: 'Children's books are an expression of my overflowing love for animals . . . By leveraging my profession as a children's books writer, I can help raise awareness of animal rights problems. If I can contribute to saving even one life, it gives me *yarigai* (value of doing). Volunteering even makes me feel that I am glad to be born into this world.'

Through her volunteering work, she found peers who are as passionate about the topic as she is. Having interests outside of work, such as hobbies and volunteering, gifts us with another way to connect and contribute to society, and allows us to feel a sense of *ikigai*.

興味関心と生き伊斐

CHAPTER 4

WORK AND IKIGAI

仕事と生き甲斐

Work and *ikigai*

Work and life in balance

The phrase 'work–life balance' has been
over-used to the point that we throw it around
without putting much thought into what
it actually means. Balance could suggest a
50/50 split, but most of the time in life, no
such thing is possible. At critical times — and
depending on the nature of your job — you
may need to devote yourself 100 per cent to
work, while at other times, you will need to
prioritize family, and work will come second.
It's also very hard to completely separate work
and life, because work is a *part* of our lives, just
as our family, friends and hobbies are. It can't
be treated as a completely separate thing.

There is nothing wrong with seeing work
as simply a means to meet financial needs, but
when you consider how much of your time
is spent at work every week, it is worthwhile

生き甲斐

finding *ikigai* in your work to keep yourself motivated in the long run.

Finding *ikigai* at work

As we have seen, *ikigai* is about paying attention to detail — breaking down life into small moments — and the same approach can be taken for work. Instead of viewing your job as a one big thing, try breaking it down into different components to discover what elements of your work bring you joy or motivate you. When someone is being negative and says 'My life sucks,' he or she is taking an all-or-nothing approach, forgetting about the good things in life and focussing only on the negatives. The same is true for work. Even if your work is less than ideal, if you look carefully, there must be some element of your work that you enjoy. Avoid taking that all-or-nothing approach, as it prevents you from finding room to improve and change your work for the better. So next time you catch yourself thinking 'My job sucks!', try reframing it. Acknowledge that perhaps you don't really enjoy the element of your work you are thinking about in that moment, but remember to reflect on the elements that you do enjoy, whether that is the sense of teamwork you get from working with your colleagues, or the feeling of achievement when you meet a deadline.

In a 2015 study on motivation at work (or *yarigai*), about 60 per cent of the 8,156 Japanese workers surveyed listed being thanked as a major motivator, while 45 per cent cited successfully accomplishing a job or a task at hand.[8] In another Japanese survey[9], women in their twenties also ranked being thanked or praised by their boss or *senpai* (older mentor) as their motivation. Japanese culture and people are known for their hospitality, and this survey reveals that even at work, they are driven by being useful to others. In relation to work and career, the word *yarigai* (value of doing) is often used to describe people's motivations at work. Surveys about *yarigai* are very common in Japan, and provide us with an opportunity to reflect on why we work and what aspects of work motivate us more than others. If being thanked is your motivator, how would you achieve that? When I first became a freelancer, I tried to give without asking for anything in return. If someone

生き甲斐

wanted me to make an introduction, I would do it as long as I thought it would be beneficial to both parties. Not only would they thank me, but what goes around comes around, and the people I had helped out would lend me a hand when I needed one. No matter how small a deed, I always show my appreciation when someone does something for me (even if it was part of that person's job). If being appreciated is what motivates you at work, you can start by first thanking others for their actions.

In my twenties, I was very eager to grow and wanted approval from people I worked with. Before I became a freelance journalist, I worked at four different companies. Each new job provided me with new ideas and skills to learn, as well as new people to interact with, but my favourite workplace was my first job, a tech startup just shy of ten people at the time I joined. I stayed there for almost five years and by the time I left, there were more than 50 employees. With them, I shared the toughest times as well as the experience of building a product (and the company) from scratch. Together, we witnessed the company grow, and the challenges we faced made us stronger as a team. I could not wait to get up in the morning to spend another day working with my teammates. Knowing where my motivation lay kept me going, no matter how tough the job got.

In a survey conducted in 2016, 82 per cent of the 5,000 Japanese men and women who responded felt that they needed to feel joy at work in order to feel fulfilled[10]. This sounds like a given, but the unfortunate reality is that although we seek joy in work, we are rarely handed our dream job. And the fact is that the company you're working for is not solely responsible for finding you a perfect job. Not only does every job come with its own set of difficulties, so no job is ever perfect, but also, it is your responsibility to tailor your work to make it as meaningful as possible.

In the same study, 74.4 per cent of those surveyed responded that by being proactive they themselves can find joy in work instead of just accepting what they are handed. They indicated that they were willing to adapt their jobs to find *ikigai* in their professional life.

生き甲斐

Job crafting

Actively shaping your job to make it a better fit to your motives, strengths and passions is called job crafting. It is the act of crafting and designing your own job instead of passively taking the job that was given to you. The term 'job crafting' was coined in 2001 by Jane Dutton and Amy Wrzesniewski.[11] Professor of Business Administration and Psychology at the University of Michigan in the US, Professor Dutton says that the idea of job crafting is not new and employees have been doing it for many years. She found that nearly 75 per cent of the workers she studied had already made small spontaneous changes or adjustments to their jobs in order to satisfy their personal needs and make their jobs more fulfilling. Finding *ikigai* at work often requires us to do some form of job crafting to make our jobs more engaging and rewarding.

When I heard the term job crafting, the first thing that came to my mind was a speech I had heard in Chicago by the *New York Times* bestselling author and Wharton Management Professor Adam Grant.[12] He mentioned a research study by economist Michael Housman that aimed to figure out why some customer service agents stayed in their jobs longer than others.[13] The fascinating link he discovered was that those who stayed longer used Firefox and Chrome as their web browsers. It was not, of course, the browser itself that kept these people in the job, but rather the fact that these employees had taken action to download a browser that was better suited for them. The default browser on a Windows computer is Internet Explorer, while on a Mac it is Safari. Almost two thirds of the customer service agents had used the default browser without ever questioning whether a better one might be out there. The longer-staying employees, however, had chosen not to simply take their job — and the tools to do it — as handed to them but rather to tweak parts of it to tailor it to their needs. This is not to say that one web browser will make you happier than another! What is important is that it shows that they took a proactive approach of questioning the default, and that customizing their job enabled them to be happier at work, which resulted in shorter call times and boosted their sales performance.

生き甲斐

Changing your perception

If you can't find meaning in your work, it will be difficult for you to see work as your *ikigai*. But whether or not you find that meaning depends not only on the tasks you have to perform but also – and perhaps particularly – on how you perceive your work. Reframing your perception of work is an essential part of job crafting and is called cognitive crafting.

In Japan, bullet trains run with meticulous precision, on some major routes as frequently as every three minutes. Here, you can witness an incredible feat performed by the bullet-train cleaners. According to an article about cleaning teams at East Japan Railway Company[14], each of a total of 22 cleaners is responsible for an entire 100-seat carriage of each train, and they are required to finish their job in a mere seven minutes. And I can testify to the impeccable cleaning job they do. If they thought of themselves as just cleaners, their motivation might be limited to doing the minimum they could get away with. But the way they see it, they are in the hospitality (or *omotenashi*, as Japanese call it) business: they are responsible for providing a pleasurable

仕事と生き甲斐

experience to travellers on bullet trains. It took a lot of changes, including things like modernizing the uniform, to transform the way in which the cleaners perceived their job, but they now take pride in their role, and knowing why they do what they do and for whom allows them to feel *ikigai* in their work. If *ikigai* can be found in the simple task of cleaning, there is no reason why you can't find it in your job, too.

Seeing the impact

For Japanese people, for whom being useful to others and being thanked for their work is a number-one motivator, interactions with people they work with or work for is crucial. This has been proved in the case of the bullet-train cleaners, who are able to see the faces of travellers stepping onto the train they have just cleaned. But it is true not only of the Japanese. Seeing the difference and the impact you are making through your work is a key to feeling motivated. In one research paper titled 'Outsource Inspiration'[15], Professor Grant explains that what motivates employees is 'doing work that affects the wellbeing of others' and to 'see or meet the people affected by their work'. In one study of cold callers at the University of Michigan, callers who met the recipient of the scholarship they're trying to raise money for raised 171 per cent more money when compared to callers who did not.[16]

As part of my research for this book, I interviewed Professor Dutton about job crafting. She told me that when she studied cleaners at the Cancer Centre at the University of Michigan in 2001, she discovered that they were job crafting by making marginal changes to the tasks they were carrying out, because they knew that something as simple as how they cleaned a faucet could ultimately affect the health of the patients. The cleaners could see who they were doing their work to benefit and the impact they were making, giving them a sense of *ikigai* even in the simplest of tasks.

As a freelance journalist, I write for many outlets, both online and offline. The readers differ depending on the media and it is exciting to be able to reach different types of people. However, it is not easy to get a 'feel' for readers when they are talked about in terms of demographics. Descriptions such as 'businessmen in the technology industry' or 'young working women in their thirties' gives me an idea of who I am writing for, but nothing beats a personal story. When a stranger who has read one of my articles writes to me about the impact it made in their lives, I realize the difference I'm making, which allows me to feel *ikigai* and reminds me of why I do what I do.

Asking yourself the right questions

In our interview, Professor Dutton told me that the first task in successful job crafting is becoming aware of how you are currently doing your work. She explained that you can do this by simply keeping a log to help you examine your working habits and asking yourself questions, such as those below. I've expanded on Professor Dutton's questions to show how you can focus your attention on each one.

- **What tasks am I doing?** No matter how small, keep a log of what you do throughout the day.
- **How do I feel about these tasks?** During each task, whether it is keeping notes at a meeting or taking a conference call with a client, pay attention to how you are feeling.

Are you enjoying these tasks? Or is it something you just want to get over with?

- **How am I spending my time?** For each task, keep track of how much time you are spending on it. Are you spending a substantial amount of time on a single task that you don't necessarily enjoy?
- **Who am I talking to or connecting to virtually or in reality?** Professor Dutton believes that one of the most powerful ways of job crafting is relational crafting. Humans are born to collaborate, not compete. So your connections in the workplace and who you are interacting with are probably related to your emotions while at work. Are you lacking interactions, or are certain interactions impacting on you in a negative way?

These questions might seem trivial, but the point is to be more aware of what you are doing and how you feel about it. Once you've mapped out your work, think about one small action you could take in each of those areas that would appeal to you, that would make you happier or more motivated. The next step is experimenting by carrying out the action.

Did it work? Did it move you along a path you wanted? If the adjustment worked, reflect this in your work.

According to Professor Dutton, you can do this alone, but asking these questions together with a colleague might help you as a team to find ways to job craft. Someone might actually enjoy a task that you dread (and therefore spend too much time on because it's a struggle) and vice versa, in which case it might be possible and probably more efficient (for the two of you, as well as for your employer) to swap tasks with each other. So if you really dislike taking minutes in meetings, but your colleague enjoys it because they find it helps them to concentrate better, it is worth finding out if minute-taking can become their responsibility, and in return you can take on another task where you can be more effective.

Finding room for creativity

Professor Dutton says that job crafting is about finding room for creativity and a continuous experimentation. The changes might not be dramatic, but a little shift here and there might just allow you to see your work as *ikigai*. And even if your *ikigai* ends up being something away from the workplace, these steps should still help you to find more fulfillment in your job.

CHAPTER 5

INSPIRING IKIGAI

Inspiring *ikigai*

In this chapter, I share with you interviews with six Japanese people about their *ikigai*. Not everyone knows what their *ikigai* is or how to phrase it in a simple way, but having a core *ikigai* in your life can mean that everything you do ends up contributing to your *ikigai* in one way or another. The people I've selected all have respectable careers and, in a general sense, would be considered successful. But they are successful not primarily because they have attained a substantial income or status (while that may be true, it is irrelevant here), but rather because they have found their true *ikigai* in life. They have chosen to pursue their *ikigai* because it fulfills them, not for material gain or to earn status or praise from society.

These people have not only shared their *ikigai* with us but also insights on how you might be able to find your own. I hope you find them inspirational.

生き甲斐

1. Rika Yajima
Founder of Japanese manufacturer aeru

At the age of 19, Rika Yajima's strong interest in Japanese traditional crafts took her all over Japan as a writer for a magazine column, during which time she built up a network of artisans. Four years later, in 2011, she founded her company, aeru, a brand of traditional Japanese products for children aged 0–6 years old. She won the APEC (Asia-Pacific Economic Cooperation) BEST Award in 2017.

What is your ikigai?
My *ikigai* is to live, or aspire to live, in a beautiful world. 'Beautiful' can mean many things, including comfort and harmony, as well as something looking or feeling beautiful. In a modern world, it is a requirement for any product to be usable, but I wanted to go beyond mere utility and create products that are beautiful and comfortable as well as useful. Because by changing your bowl or chopsticks, your food could taste better. This is why I was drawn to Japanese traditional craftsmanship and why I started my company aeru. I have a

desire to live in a beautiful world and all my decisions are geared towards making that a reality: that is my *ikigai*.

**What does ikigai *provide for you and your life?*
Ikigai is what makes you feel grateful for being alive. It is accompanied by positive feelings, such as excitement or happiness. My *ikigai* is to create a beautiful world not just for myself but for society as a whole, including the many artisans that I work with. *Ikigai* is not about being assessed or valued by society — or at least, that is not where it starts. I think *ikigai* is something you do even though no one has asked you to, simply because you want to. If you pursue that, and it ends up being useful to society, you feel a stronger sense of *ikigai*. Once you find your *ikigai*, you can live in a more relaxed way.

> **❝** I think *ikigai* is something you do even though no one has asked you to, simply because you want to.

生き甲斐

Has your ikigai *changed over time?*

My *ikigai* has not changed because it is at the very core of my life. I don't think it will ever change. My company is one way of pursuing my *ikigai*, but I pursue it in my everyday life as well. I only buy things I feel are beautiful, and I try to keep my house clean, because no matter how beautiful an object is, it would be wasted in a messy room. It is my personal goal to live in a beautiful world, and my company is a way to make that dream come true. So in every moment of my life, I am living my *ikigai*. Because I have this *ikigai* at the core, my actions are always aligned with it. I am only human so I don't achieve this perfectly all the time, but I would be happy if I can manage it 80 per cent of the time. Besides, imperfection can be beautiful, too.

Has ikigai *helped you in times of difficulty?*

It is in times of difficulty that we can lose track of ourselves and end up making bad decisions. But if you have a guiding principle — in this case *ikigai* — you will be better able to make good choices. If you make decisions that go against your *ikigai*, you will lose it, and the result will likely be disappointing. You find your *ikigai* by being true to your feelings, and by making that an anchor in your life. By staying true to your *ikigai* even in times of difficulty, you will be able to make better decisions, and positive results will follow.

How did you discover your ikigai?
It has been only over the past six months or so that I have been able to summarize my *ikigai* in a few simple words: to live in a beautiful world. Everything I was doing was always related to this, but I used different phrases and words to describe it. I believe the only way to find your *ikigai* is to have a continuous dialogue with yourself. I've never stopped asking myself questions, such as why I like something or why it feels more comfortable than something else. *Ikigai* is not something you practise but something you find. You can find it because

66 I believe the only way to find your *ikigai* is to have a continuous dialogue with yourself.

you are able to feel. I think the key is to pay attention to your feelings and ask yourself why you feel the way you do. If you continue to do this, you will find your reasons and they will lead you to discover your *ikigai*.

66 *Ikigai* is not something you practise but something you find.

How does your ikigai *fit into your daily life?*

My *ikigai* is part of my daily life, including my work at aeru, where we aspire to create a more beautiful world. There are many companies in Japan with a history of more than 100 years. The reason for the longevity of these companies is rooted in the mindset of '*sanpou yoshi*' (which can be translated as 'win-win'), which has been passed on from generation to generation. It has been a belief amongst traders going back to the Edo period that everyone should benefit — seller, buyer and society. We make our business decisions based on *sanpou yoshi* because we believe that this is one way of creating a beautiful world. All my

life decisions, including ones I make at aeru,
are always aligned with my *ikigai*.

生き甲斐

2. Ryuichiro Takeshita
Editor-in-Chief, HuffPost Japan

After graduating from Keio University in Japan, Ryuichiro Takeshita worked as a journalist at newspaper company Asahi Shimbun. After attending Stanford University as a visiting scholar for a year, he led technological business development at Asahi Shimbun. He became Editor-in-Chief of HuffPost Japan in May 2016.

What is your ikigai?
My *ikigai* is to connect different worlds. In my job as Editor-in-Chief of HuffPost Japan, I pursue this by merging print and digital media. My job also involves connecting different cultures and the values of older people and younger generations. I do this not only at work but also in my personal time, for example, by reading to learn about different values and meeting people of different ages to find a way to bridge the gap between them.

What does ikigai provide for you and your life?
I don't think that *ikigai* correlates with a salary or what you are paid for. *Ikigai* motivates you

from within and is something you do because it makes you feel good. Everything I do in my everyday life is connected to my *ikigai*. For instance, I recently taught some high-school students how to write and edit stories. I spent about 20 hours in total on this project. At a first glance, it might not seem like the most efficient way to spend my time, since I was not paid and neither does it give me page views for my website, but I felt *ikigai* doing it. All the students had either stopped going to school or had been bullied, and I found a sense of purpose in using my knowledge and skills to teach them to express themselves. Learning to do so will connect them to the rest of society, which is what my *ikigai* is about. When you pursue your *ikigai* outside of your paid job, it can influence your work in the long term. I ended up writing an article about my teaching experience.

Has your ikigai *changed over time?*

My *ikigai* has not changed over time, but as I've grown older, I have been able to better frame and phrase it. But fundamentally, it remains the same.

生きゆ斐

How did you discover your ikigai?

When I was around nine or ten years old, I was living in the US. Every summer, I would return to Japan to attend school there so that I would not forget the Japanese culture and language. One time, I decided to shoot a video of American school life by having my friends speak in front of the camera. I did the same at my school in Japan and showed it to friends in both countries. My friends from the US and Japan became pen pals and that made me feel good. Again, it wasn't a homework project or something I would be graded on, but I felt happy about connecting the two cultures. It was when I looked back at my childhood that I discovered this was my *ikigai*, which I still pursue to this day. Instead of looking from the time you started your career, you might find that going back even further in your life will give you clues about your *ikigai*.

Has ikigai *helped you in times of difficulty?*

Yes. Knowing my *ikigai* allows me to make otherwise difficult decisions. One example of such a decision was when I quit my job at Asahi Shimbun (a major newspaper company) to work at HuffPost Japan in May 2016. At an established company like Asahi, jobs are seen as lifetime employment and people tend to stay until retirement. But when you know and focus on your *ikigai*, you realize that you can pursue it not just at a certain company but elsewhere as well. I think that having *ikigai* allows you to be courageous and helps you to make life-altering decisions because you know what is important to you. Compared to my previous job, I have more freedom where I am now to pursue my *ikigai* of connecting different worlds.

> 66 Knowing my *ikigai* allows me to make otherwise difficult decisions.

How does your ikigai **fit into your daily life?**
For me, the trick is to incorporate my *ikigai* into my work as much as possible, like I did by teaching the high-school students. When you do this, the distinction between work and personal life blurs and you no longer have to try to make time for activities outside of

生き甲斐

work because they are all related in one way or another.

How can others find their ikigai?

If you're not able to find your *ikigai*, maybe you should stop looking so hard. I think that *ikigai* is something that you happen to come across. You just bump into it and when you know, you know. *Ikigai* is something very internal and you pursue it even if the rest of the world wouldn't understand. *Ikigai* comes from within.

インスピレーション

3. Haruka Mera
Founder of Japanese crowdfunding site Readyfor

After graduating from Keio University, Haruka Mera went to study at Harvard. Upon returning to Japan, in March 2011, she founded Japan's first crowdfunding site, called Readyfor, at the age of 23. In the same year, she was named a World Economic Forum Global Shaper, and was the youngest Japanese person to attend the World Economic Forum Annual Meeting.

What is your ikigai?
My *ikigai* is helping other people achieve their goals. For me, *ikigai* is a mission and a responsibility to society, something I feel I have to do and take action on. It allows me to live, and it determines all my actions. I started a crowdfunding site called Readyfor when I was 23, and found passion in helping people make their dreams come true. This mission became central to my life, and everything else, including my social life, is directly or indirectly connected to this mission.

生き甲斐

What does ikigai *provide for you and your life?*
A will to live and reasons to live.

Has your ikigai *changed over time?*
My *ikigai* has remained the same since I started Readyfor. If anything, it has grown stronger.

Has ikigai *helped you in times of difficulty?*
Ikigai plays a role as an anchor for all my decision-making. There are difficulties in life that are completely out of our control, but for ones that I can do something about, knowing my *ikigai* has shaped my actions and allowed me to take on new challenges in life. I had thought about my *ikigai* before, but what really got me thinking was when I was diagnosed with a malignant lymphoma last year at the age of 30. Until then, I had never given serious thought to life and death because I was too busy pursuing my mission. Having the time to stop and think reconfirmed to me the fact that having *ikigai* is strongly related to my will to live and my values in life.

How did you discover your ikigai?

When I look back at the time I started Readyfor, I realize that I never wanted to run a company or had never intended to make my work my *ikigai*. It simply started when I felt *yarigai* (value of doing) towards helping others achieve their goals and found a tool for that called crowdfunding. So my discovery of *ikigai* began when I chose something that moved me in some way and when I did something about it. I used all my time to build Readyfor and everything I did was for Readyfor. I believe that by continuing to pursue something and delivering results, it turns into your *ikigai*. If there is a need in society for what you're doing, it will be sustainable and it will become your role in society, as well as your *ikigai*.

How does your ikigai fit into your daily life?

For me, everything in my life is an ecosystem surrounding my mission for Readyfor. So there is no clear distinction between my work life and my personal life. There is more than one way to accomplish your mission, so I do want to make time for diverse activities. That activity can be as simple as reading about management. My next challenge in life is to

生き甲斐

better manage my time and take better care of my health. I think that having a core value or *ikigai* in life will make this possible.

4. Midori Sakano
Creative Director, Skylar

In both high school and in college, Midori Sakano went to Canada and the US as an exchange student. After graduating Master of Art for Graphic Design at Marshall University, she worked as a designer at several companies. In 2012, she joined The Honest Company at an early stage and contributed to the growth of the company. She recently joined a natural perfume company, Skylar, as a creative director. Midori is the mother of thirteen-month-old daughter, Māra.

What is your ikigai?

Ever since my daughter Māra was born, she has been my *ikigai*. But my *ikigai* before she entered my life (and also now) is to set up goals for myself and to accomplish them. A recent example would be when I resigned from a job at a company where I'd worked for almost six years and took on a new job as creative director at Skylar. I was ready to step up to the next level so I sought opportunities to make it happen. Whether I actually make it or not, having goals allows me to improve myself.

When I don't have *ikigai*, I lack any motivation or passion. Because of my *ikigai*, I feel alive and happy to be.

What does ikigai *provide for you and your life?*

My daughter brings me tremendous joy — a level of happiness I had no idea existed in life. My other *ikigai* for setting and achieving goals brings me a different kind of joy. I think part of the excitement is to feel myself constantly improving, as well as finding new things about myself along the way. Challenging yourself to be better sometimes requires you to change your perspectives on things. Being a designer, I do this a lot at work, too. When something isn't quite working, you take another approach and end up discovering something new.

How did you discover your ikigai?

There was a time when I felt like doing nothing and all I wanted to do was sleep. But I realized that this very way of spending my time (of doing nothing) was giving me more stress than anything else. Not having *ikigai* made me realize how important it is for me to have a goal to work hard towards. I feel *ikigai* when I am creating something and when the output is valued by others. There is a Japanese proverb '*Suki koso mono no jouzu nare'*, which means that how much you love something determines how good you become at it. To find *ikigai*, find out what you love doing by paying attention to your feelings. Ask yourself 'When do I feel most uplifted and excited?'.

Has your ikigai changed over time?

The birth of my daughter was certainly a big change. But my *ikigai* of setting and achieving goals has always been the same as it can evolve with me. Ever since my daughter came into my life, I feel that I need to pursue this *ikigai* even more, not just for myself but for her as well. When you have children, your life is automatically less flexible. With that in mind, my next challenge is to keep pursuing both of my *ikigai*.

Has ikigai helped you in times of difficulty?

Finding *ikigai* has helped me overcome the difficult and unmotivated times of my life. *Ikigai* is not something you find overnight, but I think the key is to take action. Although I wanted to stay in bed all day, I went out and met people to get inspired. This is something I

生き甲斐

try to do on a regular basis. Another thing I do is to visit places that are a little out of the ordinary. I recharge my creative energy by doing this. Whatever helps you feel inspired, any action is better than no action.

> **66** *Ikigai* is not something you find overnight, but I think the key is to take action.

How does your ikigai **fit in your daily life?**
With a newborn to take care of, making time for anything is a challenge. I try not to do it all on my own and ask my husband to help out. I also make plans in advance to really do the things I want to do. It's also important to boost your concentration level so that you are able to tackle things in a shorter amount of time. All you can do is to make the best of whatever time is available to you.

5. Yuko Kaifu
President of Japan House, Los Angeles

After working at the Ministry of Foreign Affairs in Japan, Yuko Kaifu was transferred to the Consulate General of Japan in Los Angeles in 2001. She worked at Union Bank as a Senior Vice President of Public Relations, as well as being the Vice President at the Japanese American National Museum. She is now the President of Japan House in Los Angeles.

What is your ikigai?

After giving this a lot of thought, I would say that work is my *ikigai*. When I say work, I do not mean simply gaining the means to support myself financially, but the fulfillment and sense of achievement I get through work. When do I feel most satisfied and fulfilled at work? When I worked at the Ministry of Foreign Affairs in Japan, in a very humble way, I felt useful by being a connector between Japan and the rest of the world. When I worked as a Vice President at the Japanese American National Museum, I felt *ikigai* in closing the growing gap between Japanese Americans and Japan. Currently, as the

生き甲斐

President of Japan House in Los Angeles, which was launched by the Japanese Ministry of Foreign Affairs with an aim to nurture a deeper understanding and appreciation of Japan in the international community, I feel joy that increasing numbers of people are showing an interest in learning about Japan.

A sense of fulfillment is not limited to work. I am often asked to participate in events for the Japanese and Japanese American communities. Sometimes the events are directly related to my work, but at other times not. I can't take time off from work, but if such an event takes place at the weekend or in the evening, I try my best to participate, even if that means sacrificing a relaxing evening at home. When I go and see the happy faces of the people there, I feel rewarded. Throughout my career, I think what has always motivated me is when I feel that I am making my small contribution to people or to society. Knowing that keeps me going, no matter how exhausted I might be.

What does ikigai *provide for you and your life?*
It gives me vitality to move forward. Even when I am really busy and working until late on a

daily basis with no days off, *ikigai* gives me the energy to keep moving. Knowing that I am living out my beliefs and making a difference makes all the hard work worthwhile.

66 It gives me vitality to move forward.

How did you discover your ikigai?
I don't think that there was a specific timing. But throughout my career, I think I rediscovered my *ikigai* when I made big career changes. You don't always find *ikigai* right away; it often takes time to find one at any job. When you reflect back on what you've been doing and what little contributions you can make where you are, you discover your *ikigai. Ikigai* is something you find through your experiences.

I don't think that many people continually ask themselves what their *ikigai* is. But when you live your life to the fullest and work hard, there are experiences that give you overwhelming emotions or an uplifting

生き甲斐

feeling. I think that this is very similar to feeling your *ikigai*. If something makes you feel such strong emotions, it might be something that can bring you a sense of fulfillment, of *ikigai*.

Has your ikigai *changed over time?*

I don't think that the basis of my *ikigai* has changed. My *ikigai* consists of small things like seeing someone happy. Essentially, all my work is involved with connecting different things. It may be about connecting people's minds or perhaps connecting two different cultures. But creating connections is at the basis of all my work.

Has ikigai *helped you in times of difficulty?*

The Japan House project is a very new initiative. The Japanese Government has never done anything like it before, nor has any other organisation tried anything quite the same. This means that we are facing new and unknown challenges every day. But knowing my *ikigai*, and feeling that I am being useful to others, has helped me move forward.

How does your ikigai *fit into your daily life?*

In my case, *ikigai* overlaps with work. But that does not mean that by doing more work I would feel even more fulfilled. I think taking a step back is important. For example, I do hot yoga every week, and from time to time I take myself off on an overnight trip to somewhere beautiful. Intentionally making that space and time away from work recharges me and inspires me to pursue my *ikigai*.

6. Dai Tamesue
Former field and track athlete, currently the
President of Deportare Partners

The first Japanese to receive a medal at Sprint
World Championships, Dai Tamesue holds the
Japanese record for 400-metre hurdles (at the
time of writing). He is currently the President
of Deportare Partners, working on projects
that connect sports and technology. He has
authored several books on such subjects as
philosophy of running and making a conscious
decision to give up.

What is your ikigai?
I am happiest when I am gaining a deeper
understanding of something, when I can help
strengthen other people's understandings or
perceptions of things, and when I find a new
side to myself. I believe that the only true way to
achieve this is by meeting and interacting with a
wide variety of people. I also read a lot and try to
take time to reflect on my encounters.

For example, when I lived in San Diego for
three years, I became close friends with a gay
couple. Back then, openly gay relationships
were relatively unusual in Japan and this was

the first time I'd had gay friends. As I got to know them, my world suddenly expanded. It made me see what a small world I had been living in. This realisation brought me tremendous joy.

My three-year-old son is a great source of inspiration as well. I remember a time when he was beginning to understand the concept of large and small. When I looked at his comparisons, I realized that he was only comparing things within the same categories or things he thought belonged in the same category. For example, he would compare the size of mum and dad but not a mountain and dad. There are obvious categorisations like the one my son made (human and nature), but maybe I am setting up categories in my own mind which might be preventing me from seeing things from different perspectives. Realizing this helped me broaden my vision.

My *ikigai* is to continue to change people's perceptions, including my own. That is my way of making an impact and influencing others, and if I can do this for the rest of my life, I would be a happy man.

生き甲斐

What does ikigai *provide for you and your life?*
Many athletes share a strong motivation to leave a legacy, whether that's achieving a new record or simply being remembered. For me, that's less important. I think having *ikigai* ensures that I will never be bored until the day I die. Maybe that's happiness. You keep chasing your *ikigai* and one day you just die. You live every day to your fullest, going to bed exhausted at the end of the day, falling asleep and then waking to another new day. *Ikigai* allows me to feel alive and gives my life a sense of purpose.

> **66** I think having *ikigai* ensures that I will never be bored until the day I die.

How did you discover your ikigai?
There was a clear timing for me, which was when I decided to retire as a professional athlete. But the difference between my retirement as an athlete and someone retiring after a long career was that I was still young

and had to find the next thing to do with my life. At this point, you really have to question what you've been doing because everything must come to an end.

At the time, I asked myself lots of questions about why I had become an athlete. Was it for fame? Was it for money? That's when I realized that there were two things that made me excited. The first was that by doing field and track, I was constantly changing: every day I was a different person than the day before. The second was that, hopefully, seeing me perform had some impact on other people, too. I realized that what I wanted to do as an athlete was to change or update people's understanding or perception of things, and that maybe I could do something similar to this in the next stage of my life. I asked myself whether I wanted to do this even though I had earned enough money to live happily for the rest of my life. And I knew that, yes, I wanted to keep doing this.

When you look back at your life, I think the memorable moments are the ones where your emotions were shaken up. Everyone should be able to recall at least a few moments like this in their life. There was a famous quote by Steve

生きゆ斐

Jobs, 'You can't connect the dots looking forwards; you can only connect them looking backwards'. I think this is true if you're talking about a vision, a sort of direction in your life, but *ikigai* is more about feeling alive in your everyday life. So ask yourself, at what moments in your life do you feel truly happy or fulfilled? Looking back at your life to pick up the clues and trying to connect them may give you insights into what your *ikigai* might be.

66 So ask yourself, at what moments in your life do you feel truly happy or fulfilled?

Has your ikigai *changed over time?*

When I was younger, I was happy about getting recognition from people. Every day, I was eager to do my workout, and sometimes I was rewarded, other times I wasn't. But around the time of my retirement at the age of 34, I was injured, and it became harder and harder for me to rely on achieving my athletic goals. That's when I changed how I look at things;

instead of focussing just on my goals, I paid attention to smaller changes I was making every day. I guess the underlying source of fulfillment was always the same for me.

Has ikigai *helped you in times of difficulty?*

For athletes, the odds of being rewarded for hard work come once a year, or four times a year, at competitions. This is fine when you're young and improving day by day, but there will be times when you hit the ceiling of growth and you feel stuck. For me, this started to happen when I was 25 or 26 years old. Like I said, this was the time when I started to look at my daily changes and achievements rather than merely at the bigger goal. If I hadn't been able to do this, the slump would have been much more difficult to overcome. When you can't climb higher by looking at the top of the mountain, look at the road you're walking on and take one step at a time; the difficult times will end at some point. I don't know if you can call this *ikigai*, but for me, instead of working backwards from where you want to be, it works to pay attention to everyday feelings.

生き甲斐

How does your ikigai *fit into your daily life?*

If you think about *ikigai* outside of work, one characteristic of it is that it makes you look forward; it's something that gets you excited for tomorrow. When you think backwards and ask yourself what makes you feel most excited, I think we spend a lot of time on things that are inessential to our happiness. So for me, what's important is to determine what my most fulfilling time is and to lock it down in my schedule. I do this at work by blocking out time in my calendar. Because a certain time is blocked, the rest of my schedule gets hectic, but by having that time to myself, I can use it to meet new people or to reflect on things. Don't think of it as making time for your *ikigai,* but prioritize that before anything else. Time to pursue your *ikigai* should come first because *ikigai* is food for your life.

CHAPTER 6

IKIGAI IS THE ACTION WE TAKE IN PURSUIT OF HAPPINESS

アクションを
ともなう
生き甲斐

Ikigai is the action we take in pursuit of happiness

Ultimately, *ikigai* is about knowing yourself.
As I have written in the very beginning of this
book, your *ikigai* shows your values in life, what
you care most about and what you prioritize.
Finding your *ikigai* is no easy task, but without
knowing what it is, you can't fulfill it — so it is
worth undertaking the search.

I feel *ikigai* when . . .

In Japanese, the word *ikigai* is mainly used
in two ways. One way refers to the object of
ikigai and the other refers to the state of mind
of feeling *ikigai*. In a sentence, they can be
phrased like this:

'I feel *ikigai towards* . . . '

and

'I feel *ikigai when* . . .'

生き甲斐

In my case, I feel *ikigai* towards writing and I feel *ikigai* when I make positive influence on people through my writing. Since having a positive influence on people is one of my values, I might enjoy other ways of achieving this besides writing, such as teaching or speaking at public events. Attempting to fill in the two sentences helps you to see beyond just the object of your *ikigai* but also to see the values behind it.

Keep an open mind

A common situation where many Japanese people feel lost is when they retire from work at the end of their career. I think this is because for many, some aspect of work has provided them with *ikigai*. When you no longer have to set your alarm clock before going to bed, or greet your colleagues in the morning, you may find yourself at a loss.

But knowing your *ikigai* or the values that lie beneath your *ikigai* will help you discover other ways to feel fulfilled at your next stage in life. If being thanked by others is a motivator for you, as it is for many Japanese workers, you can look for activities that use your knowledge and skills to support others, such as volunteering (see page 42). *Ikigai* doesn't have to be pursued in one defined situation or environment. The object of your *ikigai* can change as well. As long as you keep an open mind, your *ikigai* can find a new outlet.

Look at what you know

Looking for your *ikigai* is more like taking a slow stroll in your own neighbourhood than embarking on an unknown adventure. You may not have to look very far. Looking at both our current life and our past provides us with clues about what our *ikigai* might be. When you look, do not limit yourself to the start of your career — look as far back as your childhood. When I think about it, my *ikigai* was already apparent back in elementary (primary) school. No clear-cut moment existed, but writing (even essay assignments at school that kids tend to dread) was a consistent source of joy for me even as a child.

生き甲斐

Questions to connect the dots

For those of you who don't know where to start, here is a list of questions you can ask yourself to identify your *ikigai*. Since finding one's *ikigai* is often about connecting the dots, I have listed the questions in a timeline from the past to the future.

Ask yourself:
- Going back to my childhood, what did I enjoy the most? What events or incidents do I remember strongly? Does it still affect me today?
- Looking back at my life, what were the memorable moments where my emotions were stirred?
- What brings happiness to my everyday life?
- When do I feel happiest?
- What is the most fulfilling way that I spend my time?
- What puts a smile on my face just thinking about it?
- When have I experienced strong emotions? When do I find myself moved, and by what?
- Where does my curiosity lie?
- What keeps me from being bored?

- What aspects of my life do I seek change in?
- What is something I do even though no one asks me to?
- What would I still pursue even if the rest of the world didn't understand?
- What would I continue to do even if I had enough money to live happily ever after?
- What events do I look forward to in the future?
- What changes do I wish for in the future? What can I do about them?
- What makes me want to be alive to see tomorrow?

Take your time answering these questions. When you are finished, look at your answers. You might see a pattern emerging — one or more themes that occur again and again. Half-forgotten childhood memories might take on a whole new meaning when you consider them alongside the things that stir your curiosity or make you feel excited now.

生き甲斐

About time

When trying to identify your *ikigai*, it also helps to pay more attention to how you are spending your time. Having become used to our overly busy lives, our minds are on autopilot, not thinking twice before cramming plans into our schedule. This prohibits us from acknowledging how we are spending our time or seeing any sort of patterns that might exist. Be mindful when you are making plans and take some time to go over your past activities as well as your future plans. Remember that *ikigai* is often accompanied by action.

What did you **do** and how did it make you **feel**?

What are you **making time for** and how much are you **looking forward** to it?

When your *ikigai* finds you

Once you know your true *ikigai*, it will act as an anchor for your decision-making, enabling you to make more solid and confident decisions. Another thing is that when you are aware of your *ikigai* (or have a better idea of what it might be), anything that might be connected to it seems to magically find its way to you, as if some unknown force is trying to encourage you to pursue it.

Here is an example. Up until now, most of my writing has been in Japanese, but the idea of writing regularly in English has come to mind multiple times in my career. I often thought that, if I were to write in English, I would want to write about my country and my culture to help other people to understand them better. Although I had not actively sought out this idea, it was always lingering somewhere in my mind. And by being aware of this 'potential *ikigai*', it attracted me to the resources for this book long before any talk of publication took place.

Believe it or not, some of the books I've referenced in this book were books I already had at home. I had picked them up on random occasions in the past, even though at the time I had no idea that I would be writing a book on *ikigai* and that they would provide perfect research material for it. But when I skimmed through these books at the bookstore, something about them struck a chord with me.

What if, when I was at the bookstore, the covers and the titles of these books hadn't

生きゆ斐

grabbed my attention? What if, when I saw these books, I had dismissed the tingle of curiosity that rose inside me? Luckily each of these books did grab my attention and I did reach out for them.

I think the lesson here is that when you find anything even remotely interesting, try not to dismiss it so easily. By dismissing your subtle interests, you are missing your chance to find out if it's something transient or if there is anything more to it. Pay attention to the things that pique your interest and give them a chance to develop into something more.

The action we take

After talking to many people about their *ikigai* and putting my thoughts in writing, I believe that happiness is a result of having or feeling *ikigai*. There is no right or wrong answer to what *ikigai* is to a person, but one thing we can say for sure is that you can't find your *ikigai* by sitting around the house. Because *ikigai* is the action we take in pursuit of happiness.

References

1. Mitsuhashi, Y., 'Ikigai: A Japanese concept to improve work and life', *BBC*, 7 August 2017, http://www.bbc.com/capital/story/20170807-ikigai-a-japanese-concept-to-improve-work-and-life

2. Survey on *ikigai*, Central Research Services, 2010, http://www.crs.or.jp/backno/No636/6362.htm

3. Kamiya, M., *Ikigai-ni-tsuite (About Ikigai)*, Misuzu Shobo, 1966.

4. Buettner, D., *The Blue Zones: Lessons on Living Longer from the People Who've Lived the Longest*, Washington DC, National Geographic, 2008.

5. Buck, P.S., *The People of Japan*, London, Robert Hale, 1968.

6. Pilling, D., *Bending Adversity: Japan and the Art of Survival*, London, Penguin, 2014.

7. Survey on hobbies outside of work, SonyLife, 2013, http://www.sonylife.co.jp/company/news/25/nr_130925.html

8. Survey on *yarigai* at work, En-Japan, 2015, http://bit.ly/2rV8UG6

9. Survey of women in their 20s about *yarigai* at work, En-Japan, 2014, http://bit.ly/2FuHwAL

10. Survey about joy at work, Recruit Career, 2016, http://bit.ly/2nJMl0B

11. Wrzesniewski, A. and J. Dutton, 'Crafting a Job: Revisioning Employees as Active Crafters of Their Work', *The Academy of Management Review*, vol. 26, no. 2, 2001, http://bit.ly/2GxHsBU

12. Grant, A.M, 'Who Are the Originals? Lessons Learned From the People Who Champion Novel Ideas and Build Cultures of Non-Conformity', *Oracle HCM World*, Chicago, April 2016.

13. 'The Maddest Men of All', *Freakonomics,* [podcast], Freakonomics Radio, 2015, http://bit.ly/2DORltb. Also see: Pinsker, J., 'People Who Use Firefox or Chrome Are Better Employees,' *The Atlantic*, 16 March 2015, http://theatln.tc/2GwQ8IL

14. Article on bullet train cleaning company TESSEI, *NewsPicks*, August 2017, https://newspicks.com/news/2278752/body/

15. Grant, A.M., 'Outsource Inspiration', available from: http://whr.tn/2wK1a8z. Also see: Grant, A. M., & D.A. Hofmann,

'Outsourcing inspiration: The performance effects of ideological messages from leaders and beneficiaries', *Organizational Behavior and Human Decision Processes*,vol. 116, 2011, pp. 173-187.

16. Grant, A. M., et al., 'Impact and the art of motivation maintenance: The effects of contact with beneficiaries on persistence behavior', *Organizational Behavior and Human Decision Processes*, vol. 103, 2007, pp. 53-67. Available from: http://whr.tn/2wK1a8z

生き甲斐

Index